D0578096

The
Nature
Treasury

A First Look at the Natural World

Written by

LIZANN FLATT

Illustrated by

Allan Cormack and Deborah Drew-Brook

Maple Tree Press Inc.
51 Front Street East, Suite 200, Toronto, Ontario M5E 1B3
www.mapletreepress.com

Text © 1994, 2005 Maple Tree Press
Illustrations © 1994, 2005 Allan Cormack and Deborah Drew-Brook, except illustrations in
upper right corner of pages 13, 21, 27, 35, and 39 which are © 1994, 2005 Jock McRae

All rights reserved. No part of this book may be reproduced or copied in any form without
written consent from the publisher.

Distributed in Canada by Raincoast Books
9050 Shaughnessy Street, Vancouver, British Columbia V6P 6E5

Distributed in the United States by Publishers Group West
1700 Fourth Street, Berkeley, California 94710

Cataloguing in Publication Data
Flatt, Lizann
    The nature treasury: a first look at the natural
world/Lizann Flatt; illustrated by Allan Cormack and
Deborah Drew-Brook.

First published under title: My first nature treasury.
ISBN 1-897066-42-2

    1. Nature—Juvenile literature. 2. Natural history—
Juvenile literature. I. Drew-Brook-Cormack, Allan
II. Drew-Brook-Cormack, Deborah III. Title.

QH48.F59 2005   j508   C2005-900705-2

Design & art direction: Wycliffe Smith (interior), Claudia Dávila (cover)
Illustrations: Allan Cormack, Deborah Drew-Brook, and Jock McRae

We acknowledge the financial support of the Canada Council for the Arts, the Ontario Arts
Council, the Government of Canada through the Book Publishing Industry Development
Program (BPIDP), and the Government of Ontario through the Ontario Media Development
Corporation's Book Initiative for our publishing activities.

ONTARIO ARTS COUNCIL
CONSEIL DES ARTS DE L'ONTARIO

Printed in China

A   B   C   D   E   F

Contents

Exploring Nature

From the tiniest flower to the largest whale, every living thing on our planet is a part of nature. Exploring nature means discovering a new mix of living things everywhere you look.

Have you ever been to a desert? How about to the Arctic or to the bottom of the ocean? Well, we are going to take you there so that you can see the amazing plants and animals that live in these places. You'll climb in the tree habitats; a forest and a rain forest. You'll roam the grasslands; prairie, savanna and tundra. You'll wander across a harsh and hot desert. Then you'll dive down into the water to explore a lake, a river, an ocean and a coral reef.

Along the way, you'll find out some incredible secrets of nature. Did you know that just a few things on Earth make it possible for all plants and animals to live? You'll get a really close-up look at water, air, trees, soil and grass. You'll discover many different families of animals and plants, what they eat, and how they grow.

And there's something special for you to do, too.

cheetah

Whenever you see animals or plants on a black circle, like these,

ground squirrel

bison

butterfly

find as many of them as you can in the picture. Look closely, they are all there somewhere.

Now, get ready for your exciting journey through nature around the world.

All Kinds of Animals

Animals are living things. They can use their senses (hearing, sight, smell, taste, touch) to take in what's around them, and they can move around whenever they choose.

Mammals feed their babies milk. Most mammals have fur or some kind of hair.

bat

lemur

zebra

whale

Birds have feathers and lay hard-shelled eggs.

goose

kiwi

eagle

Reptiles have dry scaly skin, and they have to sit in the sun or shade to warm up or cool down.

turtle

snake

alligator

Amphibians are born in the water and have moist skin.

caecilian

frog

salamander

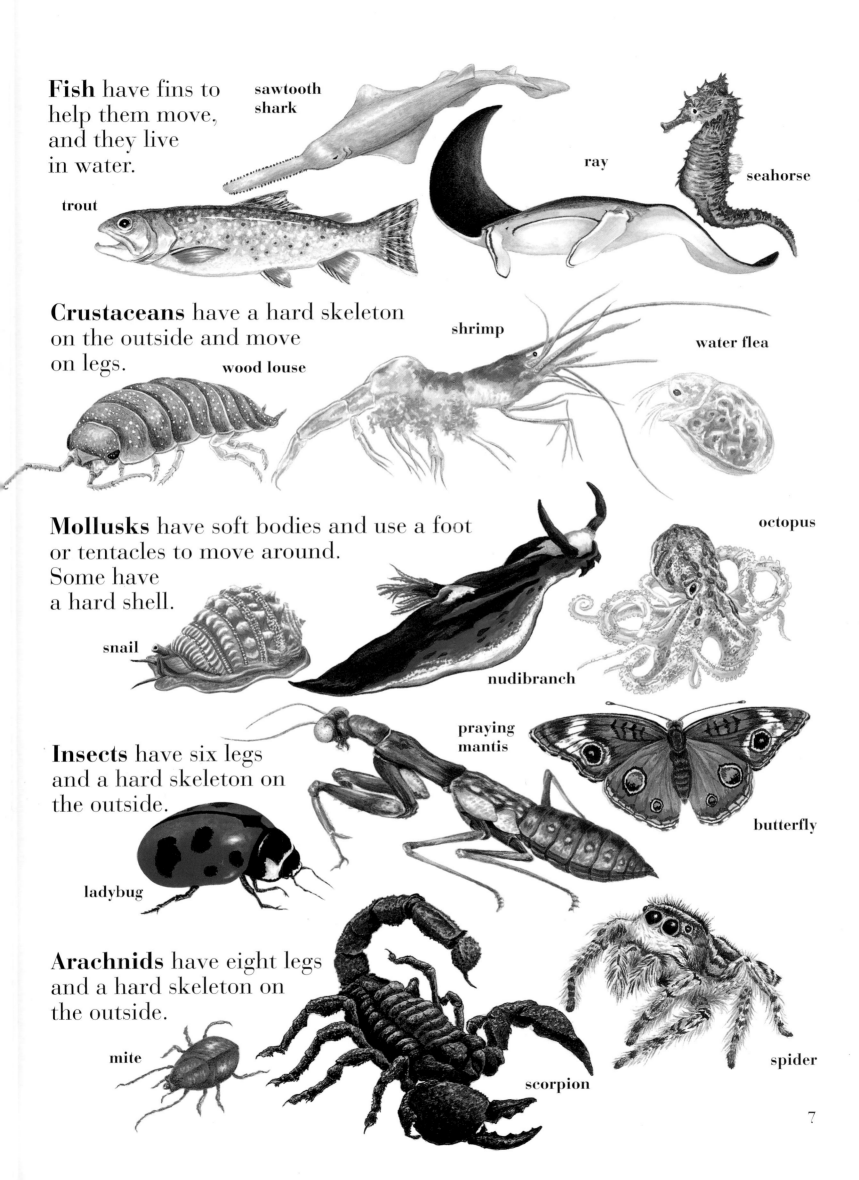

Fish have fins to help them move, and they live in water.

sawtooth shark

ray

seahorse

trout

Crustaceans have a hard skeleton on the outside and move on legs.

shrimp

water flea

wood louse

Mollusks have soft bodies and use a foot or tentacles to move around. Some have a hard shell.

octopus

snail

nudibranch

praying mantis

Insects have six legs and a hard skeleton on the outside.

butterfly

ladybug

Arachnids have eight legs and a hard skeleton on the outside.

mite

scorpion

spider

7

How Animals Grow

**Swallowtail
Butterfly**

5. At last
the chrysalis opens and out
comes a butterfly.

4. The caterpillar
sheds its outer covering
again and forms a
chrysalis. Inside the
chrysalis changes are
happening.

Start here

1. Tiny mice
are born. They're
hungry for their
mother's milk.

2. The mice grow
more hair, but they still
can't see or hear.

Start here

1. The female butterfly laid this egg. Then she flew away.

2. A little caterpillar hatches. It eats leaves to grow bigger.

3. The caterpillar crawls out of its hard outer covering many times as it grows.

Harvest Mouse

4. The grown-up mice can find food and take care of themselves.

3. Now the mice are furry. Their eyes and ears have opened.

Cardinal

4. Now the birds are all grown. They can take care of themselves.

3. The chicks are fed so they will grow. Their feathers are growing too.

Start here

1. The female crab has laid her eggs. She carries them around underneath her body.

2. The eggs hatch into tiny larvae. They float in the sunny water and eat tiny plants.

3. Each larva crawls out of its hard outer covering many times as it grows. It looks different each time.

Start here

1. The female bird has laid her eggs. She sits on them to keep them warm.

2. The little chicks hatch from the eggs. They can't see for a few days.

Blue Crab

5. The crab keeps growing bigger and bigger by crawling out of its old outer covering.

4. This baby sheds its outer covering again. Now it looks like an adult, but it's still small.

Soil Up Close

What is soil made of?

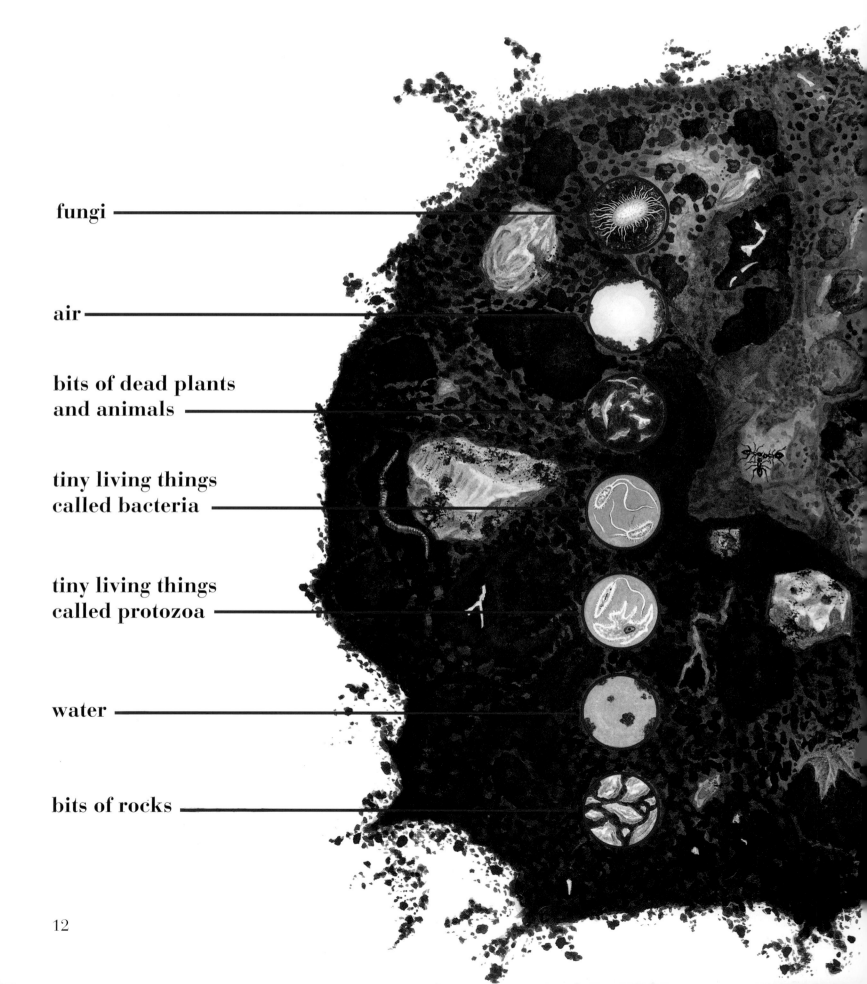

fungi

air

bits of dead plants
and animals

tiny living things
called bacteria

tiny living things
called protozoa

water

bits of rocks

Soil helps plants grow, and plants are food for animals. Some animals even live in soil.

Soil is a thin layer on top of rock.

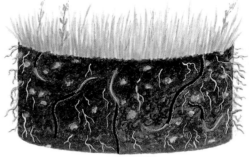
topsoil

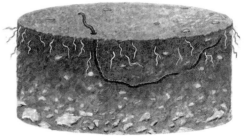
subsoil

broken rock

solid rock

All Kinds of Plants

Plants are things that are alive. They make their own food using sunshine, and they respond to changes in light, weather and other things around them.

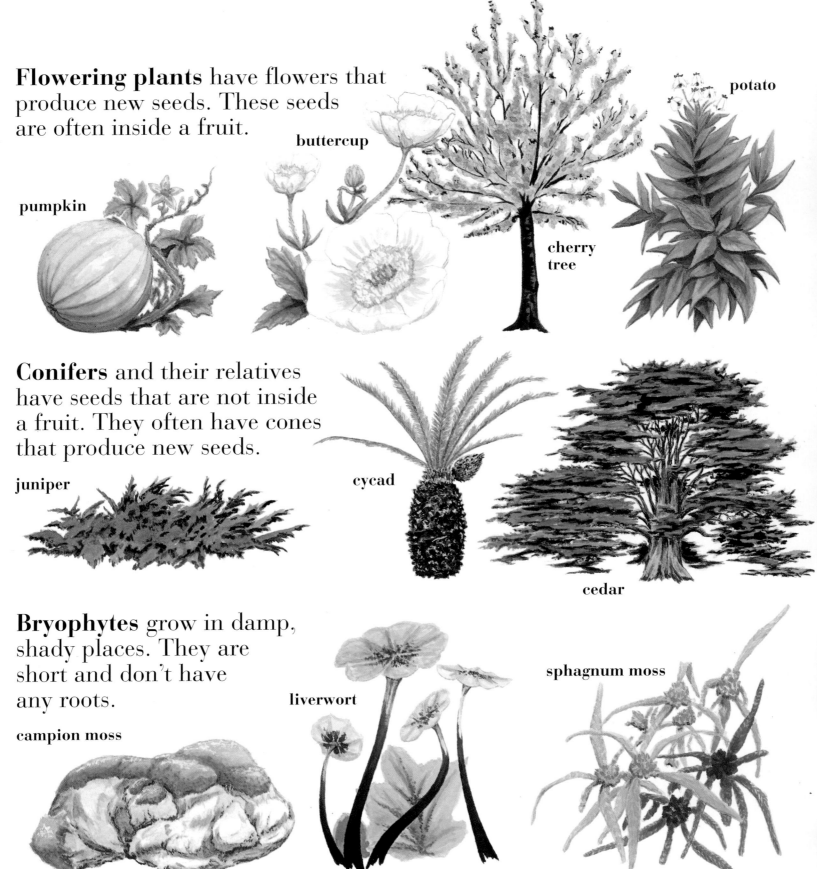

Flowering plants have flowers that produce new seeds. These seeds are often inside a fruit.

potato

buttercup

pumpkin

cherry tree

Conifers and their relatives have seeds that are not inside a fruit. They often have cones that produce new seeds.

juniper

cycad

cedar

Bryophytes grow in damp, shady places. They are short and don't have any roots.

liverwort

sphagnum moss

campion moss

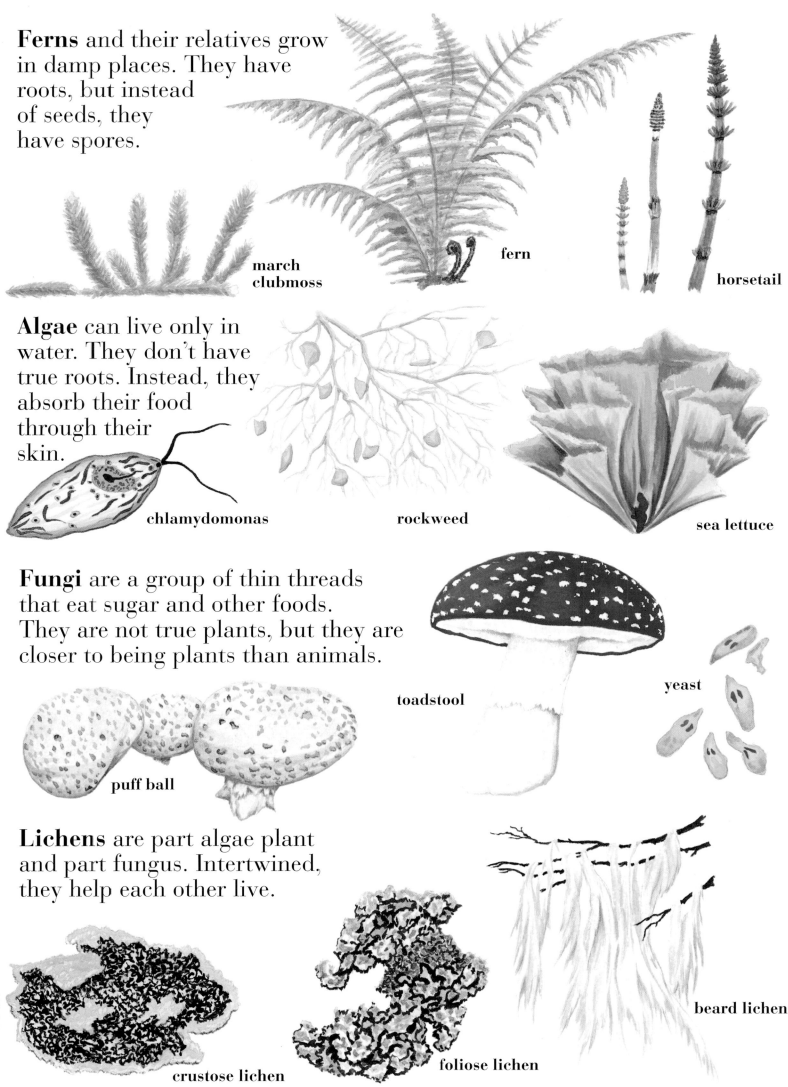

Ferns and their relatives grow in damp places. They have roots, but instead of seeds, they have spores.

march clubmoss

fern

horsetail

Algae can live only in water. They don't have true roots. Instead, they absorb their food through their skin.

chlamydomonas

rockweed

sea lettuce

Fungi are a group of thin threads that eat sugar and other foods. They are not true plants, but they are closer to being plants than animals.

toadstool

yeast

puff ball

Lichens are part algae plant and part fungus. Intertwined, they help each other live.

crustose lichen

foliose lichen

beard lichen

15

How Plants Grow

Fern

4. The fern grows bigger as more fronds uncurl. Soon more spores will form on the underside of some fronds to grow new ferns.

3. A few roots and a tall frond begin to grow. The heart-shaped plant dies.

Start here

1. The milkweed fluff floats through the air. It lands on the ground and the seed falls off.

2. Soon a small sprout peeks out of the soil. The seed cover falls off.

3. The plant grows taller. More and more leaves appear, and the flowers open.

1. A tiny spore falls off a fern. It lands in a moist, shady spot.

2. The spore grows into a small, heart-shaped plant. Underneath this plant, egg cells develop into a tiny new plant.

5. The flowers with new pollen become pods. Soon the pods will split and milkweed fluff will blow away to grow new plants.

4. Insects come to drink the sweet flower nectar, and pollen sticks to their feet. When the insects move on, the pollen sticks to other milkweed flowers.

Milkweed

What Animals Eat

All living things need food. Plants on land and in water use sunlight to make food for themselves. Some animals eat plants such as grasses and phytoplankton. Other animals eat the animals that eat those plants. Sometimes bigger animals eat *them*.

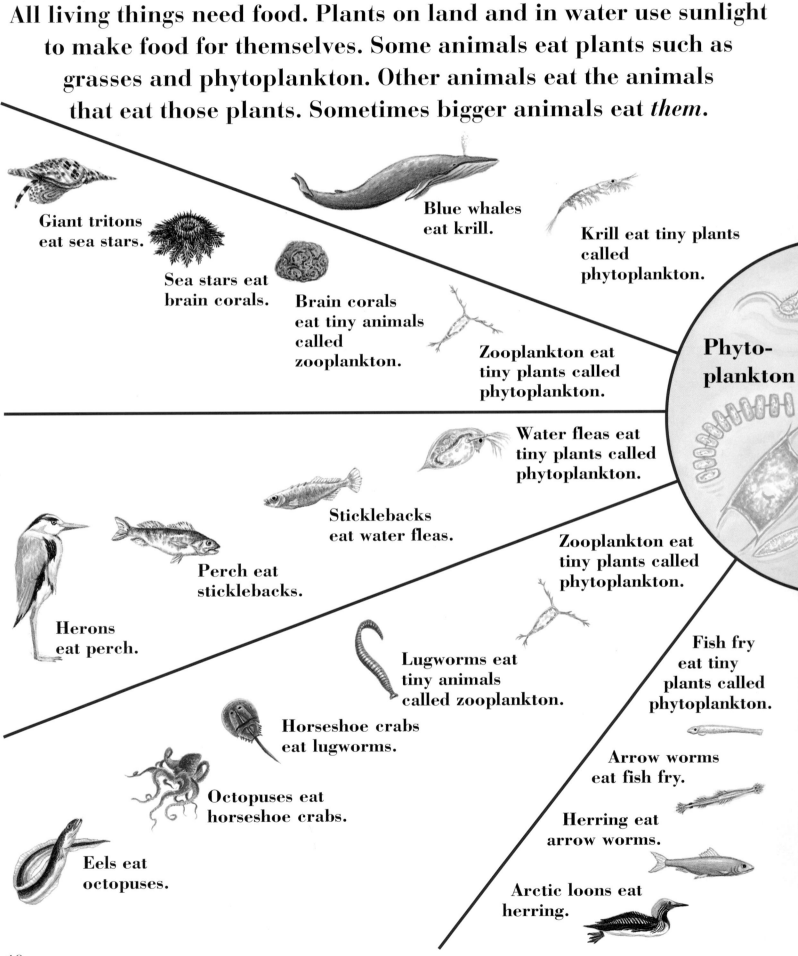

Giant tritons eat sea stars.

Sea stars eat brain corals.

Brain corals eat tiny animals called zooplankton.

Blue whales eat krill.

Krill eat tiny plants called phytoplankton.

Zooplankton eat tiny plants called phytoplankton.

Phyto-plankton

Water fleas eat tiny plants called phytoplankton.

Sticklebacks eat water fleas.

Perch eat sticklebacks.

Herons eat perch.

Lugworms eat tiny animals called zooplankton.

Zooplankton eat tiny plants called phytoplankton.

Horseshoe crabs eat lugworms.

Octopuses eat horseshoe crabs.

Eels eat octopuses.

Fish fry eat tiny plants called phytoplankton.

Arrow worms eat fish fry.

Herring eat arrow worms.

Arctic loons eat herring.

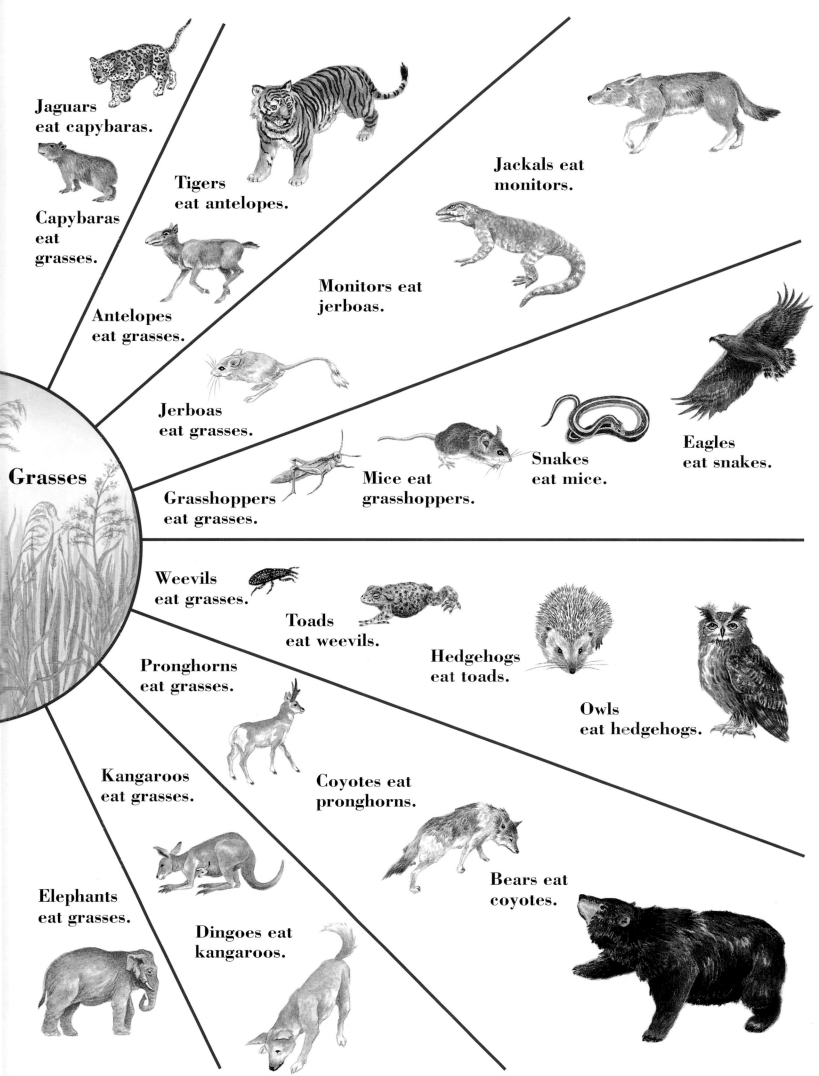

Jaguars eat capybaras.

Capybaras eat grasses.

Tigers eat antelopes.

Antelopes eat grasses.

Jackals eat monitors.

Monitors eat jerboas.

Jerboas eat grasses.

Grasshoppers eat grasses.

Mice eat grasshoppers.

Snakes eat mice.

Eagles eat snakes.

Grasses

Weevils eat grasses.

Toads eat weevils.

Hedgehogs eat toads.

Owls eat hedgehogs.

Pronghorns eat grasses.

Kangaroos eat grasses.

Coyotes eat pronghorns.

Bears eat coyotes.

Elephants eat grasses.

Dingoes eat kangaroos.

Trees Up Close

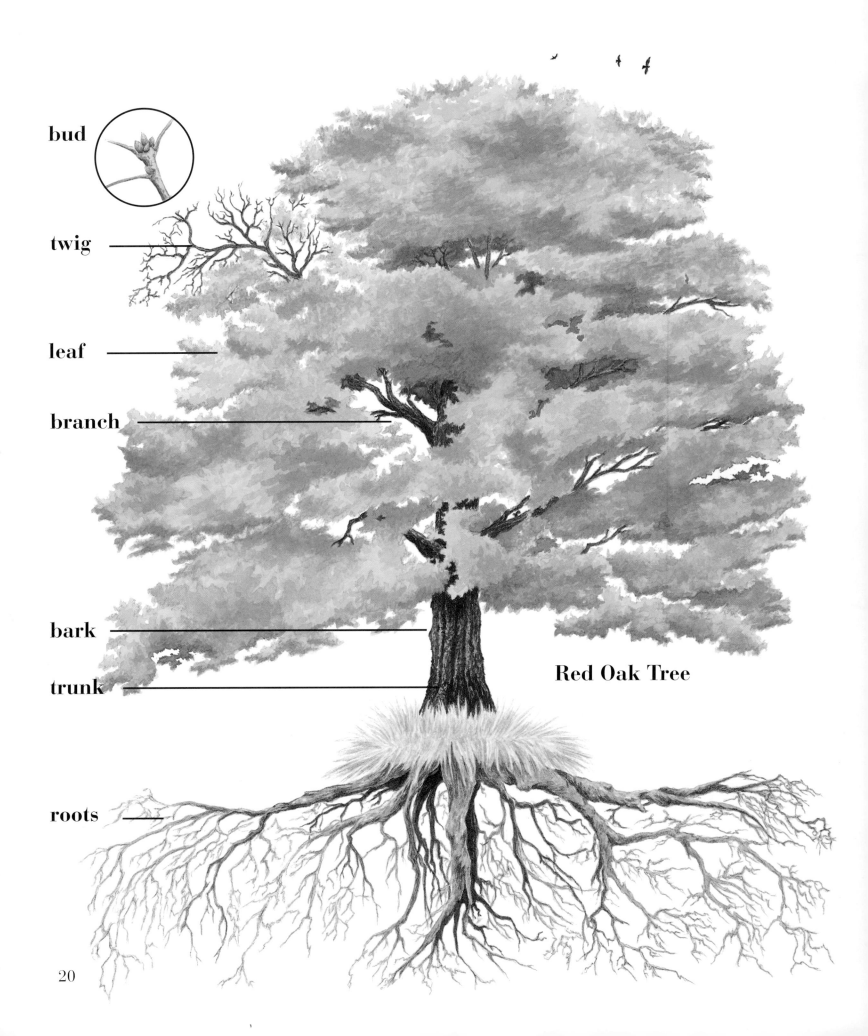

bud

twig

leaf

branch

bark

trunk

Red Oak Tree

roots

People, animals and plants
need trees for food, shade
and sometimes even
for homes. Trees clean
the air we breathe, too.

bud

needles

twig

branch

bark

trunk

roots

Red Pine Tree

Leaves can be many shapes.
Needles are leaves, too.

red oak leaf

mountain ash leaf

white cedar needles

red pine needles

white birch leaf

21

Forest

goshawk

worm

carpenter ants

garter snake

red oak

rabbit

red pine

wood frog

chickadee

22

A North American mixed forest during the day.

woodpecker **deer** **squirrel**

RECYCLED LEAVES

Millipedes, springtails
and worms eat fallen leaves.
Their bodies digest the leaves
and turn them into food for the soil.

Rain Forest

A South American rain forest during the day.

giant toad

POOL IN A TREE

Bromeliad plants grow on trees and collect rainwater. They make good homes for growing tadpoles and mosquitoes.

jaguar

agouti

tent bat

katydid

vine snake

army ant

howler monkey

harpy eagle

sloth

liana vine

hummingbird

marmoset

potoo

scarlet macaw

Grass Up Close

Kentucky Bluegrass

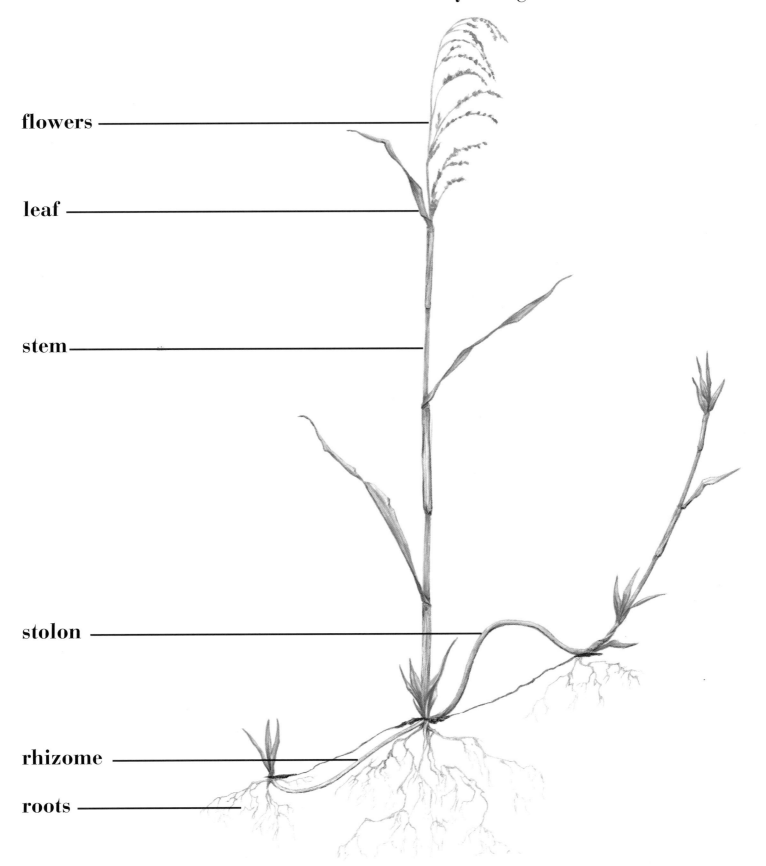

flowers ——————————————

leaf ——————————————

stem ——————————————

stolon ——————————————

rhizome ——————————————

roots ——————————————

People and animals eat grasses.

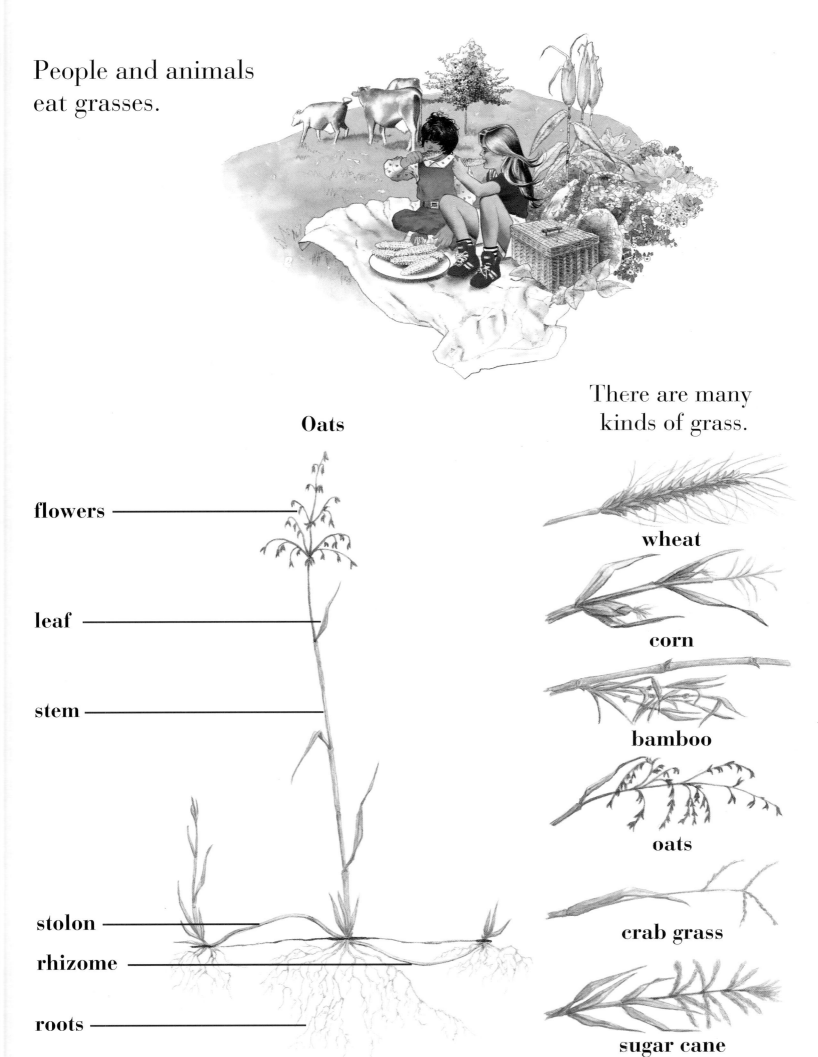

Oats

flowers ——————

leaf ——————

stem ——————

stolon ——————

rhizome ——————

roots ——————

There are many kinds of grass.

wheat

corn

bamboo

oats

crab grass

sugar cane

Prairie

ground squirrel

bison

prairie dog

buffalo grass

TUNNEL TOWN

Prairie dogs live in a group of underground tunnels called a town. They have food rooms, baby rooms and bathrooms!

The North American prairie early in the morning.

grasshopper

magpie

badger

jack-rabbit

butterfly

coyote

pronghorn antelope

bumblebee

rattlesnake

29

Savanna

red oat grass

Thomson's gazelle

termite

rhinoceros

ostrich

cheetah

secretary bird

The African savanna during the day.

lion

giraffe

hyena

SNACK ON A BACK

Oxpecker birds help other animals by eating the ticks that live on their skin and bite them.

vulture

zebra

puff adder

dung beetle

Tundra

CHANGING COLORS

Being white makes it easier to hide in snow. Animals such as the ermine, ptarmigan and arctic fox grow darker coats for summer camouflage.

caribou

arctic fox

The Arctic tundra early in winter.

polar bear

arctic hare

ermine

musk-ox

snowy owl

arctic ground squirrel

gyrfalcon

lemming

ptarmigan

lichen

blue-joint grass

raven

33

Air Up Close

**Air is made up of invisible gases that people, animals and plants breathe.
What else is in air?**

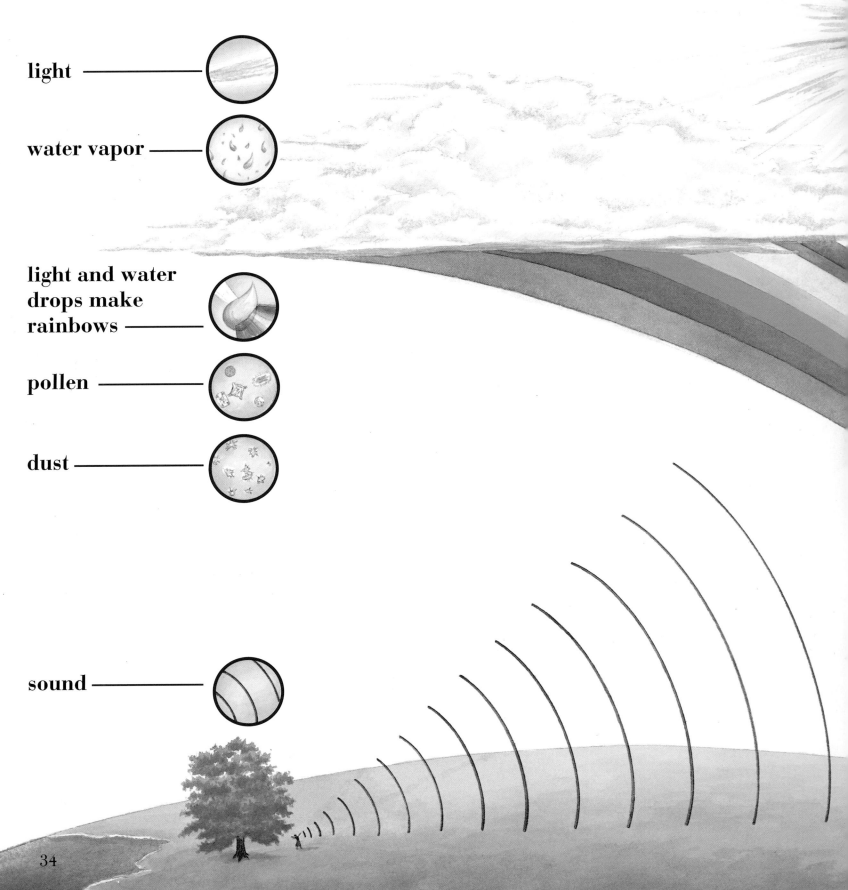

light

water vapor

light and water
drops make
rainbows

pollen

dust

sound

People, animals and plants
need air to breathe.

Air can move slowly
or quickly.

breeze

wind

gale

tornado

hurricane

Desert

desert cape hare

agama

sidewinder viper

calligonum

sedge

scorpion

hoopoe lark

oryx

The Arabian Desert in the morning.

desert locust

sand cat

camel

sand fox

houbara bustard

SEA OF SAND

The wind shapes sand into hills called dunes. Sand dunes are always being moved around, and when the wind gets really strong, it makes sand storms.

Water Up Close

What is in water?

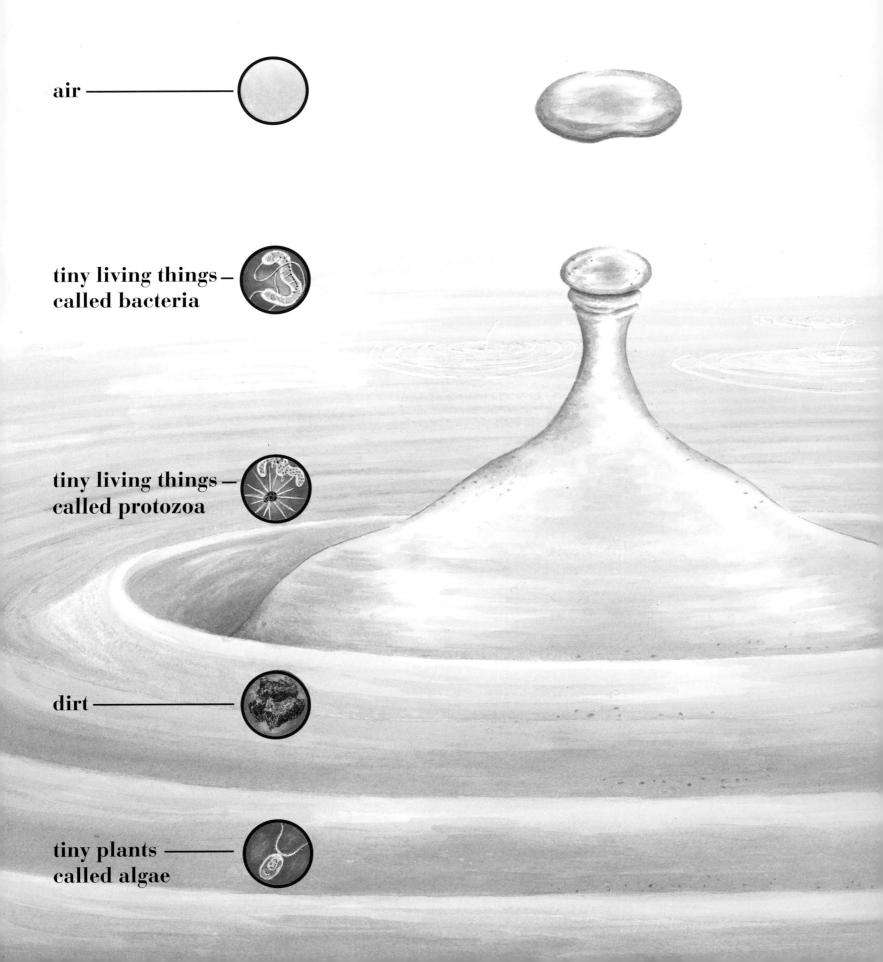

air

tiny living things — called bacteria

tiny living things — called protozoa

dirt

tiny plants called algae

People, animals and plants need water to drink.

Water comes in different forms.

clouds

rain

fog

hail

snow

Lake

fishing spider

whirligig beetle

moorhen

duckweed

dragonfly

frog

harvest mouse

newt

40

A small western European lake in the morning.

perch

stickleback

pike

A LAKE IN WINTER

Only the top of the lake freezes. Animals such as fish and frogs live under the ice during the winter.

moose

water lily

gray heron

water vole

41

River

harlequin duck

rainbow trout

river otter

dipper

WHERE RIVERS BEGIN

A river can begin as a small trickle of water. It flows until it meets a creek and makes it bigger, then that creek makes another creek bigger, and so on until the moving water becomes a river.

42

A North American river in the afternoon.

sculpin

caddis fly larva

painted turtle

water crowfoot

kingfisher

crayfish

muskrat

swallowtail butterfly

43

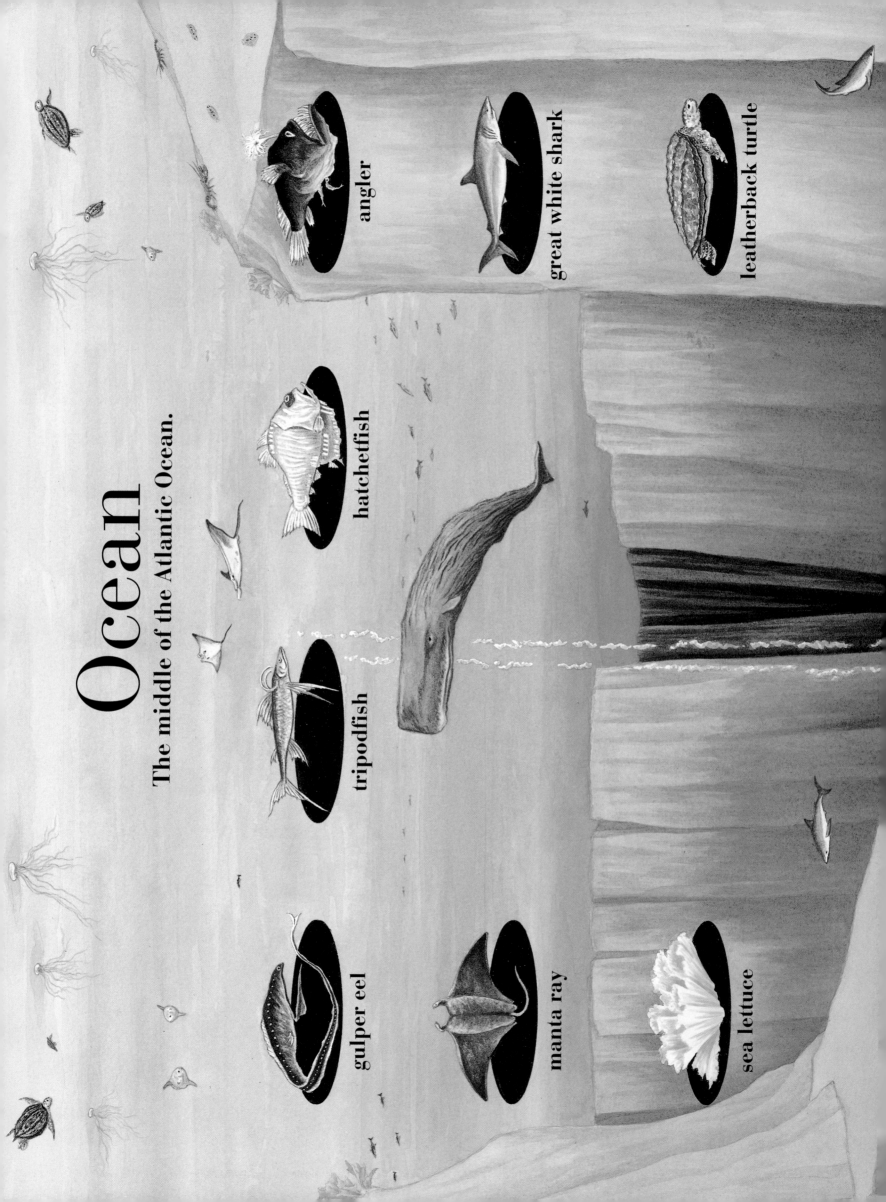

Ocean
The middle of the Atlantic Ocean.

angler

great white shark

leatherback turtle

hatchetfish

tripodfish

gulper eel

manta ray

sea lettuce

giant sunfish

MAKING CLOUDS

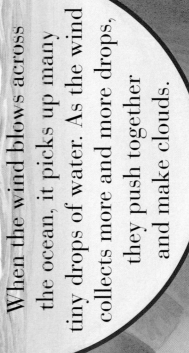

When the wind blows across the ocean, it picks up many tiny drops of water. As the wind collects more and more drops, they push together and make clouds.

Portuguese man-of-war

tuna

lobster

flounder

sperm whale

Coral Reef

sea star

potato cod

moray eel

parrotfish

clownfish

octopus

damselfish

butterflyfish

The Great Barrier Reef during the day.

flat worm

giant clam

crinoid

sea fan

CORAL AT NIGHT

Corals poke out of their hard skeletons to look for food. They wave their tentacles to find tiny floating creatures to eat.

dolphin

sea snake

brain coral

cuttlefish

47

More About ...

Algae A group of water plants that can be as small as microscopic single cells or as large as giant kelp. Every cell on each plant's surface can absorb the nutrients it needs.

Amphibians A group of animals that are cold-blooded and depend on the environment to heat and cool their bodies. Most amphibians are born and grow up in the water and live as adults on land near water.

Arachnids A group of animals that have eight walking legs, but no antennae, wings or compound eyes. Every arachnid has a pair of fang-like mouthparts in front of its mouth opening, and behind this it has a pair of leg- or pincer-like appendages.

Bacteria Microscopic single-celled life forms that grow on and inside all living things, soils and water. They may be shaped like rods, spheres or spirals.

Bryophytes A group of plants that need constant moisture. They are small and often grow along the ground in damp areas. They don't have true roots, stems or leaves.

Caecilians A type of amphibian. Caecilians have no arms or legs and their eyes, which are used to sense light, are covered by skin.

Camouflage Features of an animal's appearance that make it hard to see in its natural environment. Camouflage helps some animals hide from their enemies and helps others stay hidden as they hunt for their prey.

Chrysalis The hard case inside which a butterfly caterpillar (called a pupa at this stage) goes through metamorphosis. It emerges from the chrysalis as a butterfly.

Coral A type of animal with a tube-like body and a mouth opening surrounded by tentacles. Some corals have internal skeletons and some external. Most grow in large groups with their bodies joined together to form a colony.

Crustaceans A group of mostly aquatic animals whose bodies are covered with a hard, segmented exoskeleton. This exoskeleton must be shed through molting in order for the animal to grow.

Fungi A group of plants that are parasitic or feed off dead material. Because of their structure and because they don't make food from sunlight, they are not considered true plants.

Larva The "baby" stage of many invertebrates such as insects, crustaceans and mollusks. It is the name used for the animal from the time it is born or hatched until it is ready to change into its adult form.

Lichens A group of plants in which each individual plant is an alga and a fungus living together. Lichens usually grow on rocks and trees. The alga provides sugars for the fungus and the fungus provides water and minerals and gives the lichen its shape.

Mammals A group of animals that maintain their own body temperature and breathe air with their lungs. Mammals give birth to live babies that are fed milk from the mother's mammary glands.

Mollusks A group of legless animals that have soft bodies which in many cases are protected by a hard shell. They have a "toothed tongue" or radula and a fold of skin that forms a pocket to protect their soft parts.

Plankton Tiny plants and animals found in oceans, lakes and other bodies of water. They float near the surface of the water and use sunlight to make food. Some are larval forms of crustaceans, mollusks and other water animals.

Pollen Produced by seed-bearing plants, pollen looks like tiny grains of dust. It contains the plant's male sex cells. Flowers must come in contact with pollen from other flowers of the same kind in order to produce fruit and therefore new seeds.

Protozoa Single-celled life forms that are usually found in water or in some other liquids. Some drift, some crawl or swim, and some stay still. They are neither plants nor animals.

Reptiles A group of animals whose bodies are covered in dry scales. Reptiles depend on the environment to heat and cool their bodies. Most lay shelled eggs on land, but some give birth to live babies.

Rhizomes Thick underground stems that usually grow horizontally. New plants can develop at intervals along the length of the rhizome.

Spores Tiny reproductive cells produced by non-seed-bearing plants. Each spore can develop into a new plant.

Springtails Small animals closely related to insects, but not true insects. Springtails live in sheltered, damp places and on the surface of water. Each springtail has a forked tail that can spring downward to send the insect up into the air.

Stolons Slender horizontal stems, sometimes called runners, that grow along the surface of the ground. New plants can develop at intervals along the length of the stolon.

Tundra A northern environment that contains many bogs and small lakes. There are no trees, only small shrubs, grasses, sedges, lichens and other similar plants. The tundra is completely frozen for most of the year.